Whales
Dolphins & Seals

François Moutou

Illustrations
François Desbordes
and
Jean Chevallier
Joël Dyon

Translated by
Josephine Weightman

HarperCollins*Publishers*

COLLINS WATCH GUIDES

Black and white artwork: Alban
Larousse
Translation: Jo Weightman

ISBN 0 00 220089 9
© Éditions Gallimard, Paris, 1995
© in this translation HarperCollins*Publishers*, London, 1997
Printed and bound in Italy

Contents

● The sperm whale, which is an exceptional diver, prefers life deep in the ocean. The large fin whales, which live off filtered plankton or small fish, avoid coming near to the shore. Only the minke whale occasionally ventures close.

● Body shape, size and shape of the spout, rhythm of surfacing to breath, swimming and diving movements and social behaviour are useful criteria for identifying whales and dolphins.

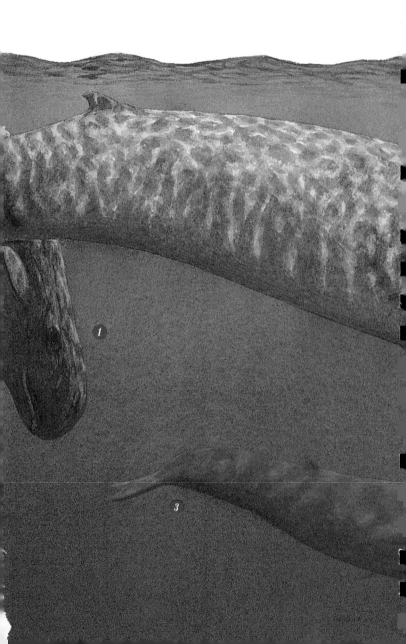

● The ocean and the seas which surround our coasts form the marine mammal world. From the grey seal to the fin whale and sperm whale, each species exploits, in its own way, resources occurring between inshore waters and the open sea.

● The marine mammals include the Cetacea (whales, dolphins, etc) and the Pinnipedia (seals, walrus, sea-lions). They all breathe air, but there is a wide range of size, biology and behaviour.

1. Sperm whale. 2. Bottle-nosed dolphin.
3. Fin whale. 4. Striped dolphin.
5. Common dolphin. 6 Grey seal.

Mammals

The coast of Western Europe is cut into a series of peninsulas. Each of these land areas offers opportunities for watching marine mammals.

● European shores are bounded by the North Sea, the Baltic Sea, the Mediterranean and the English Channel, waters criss-crossed by numerous species.

Some species to see in the Mediterranean: 1. Cory's shearwater. 2. Striped dolphin. 3. Sperm whale. 4. Fin whale.

in the Sea

Sometimes sailors come across birds, fish and mammals gathered in a frenzy at their feeding ground.

● All the species described in this book may be found in the North Atlantic.

Below: 1. Sperm whale. 2. Manx shearwater. 3. Minke whale. 4. Gannet. 5. Bottle-nosed dolphin. 6. Kittiwake. 7. Grey seal.

● Seals are strictly confined to the coast; they spend much of their life basking on shore and hunting out at sea at high tide. Females give birth on land.

● Marine mammals are good indicators of the ecological health of the seas immediately around us.

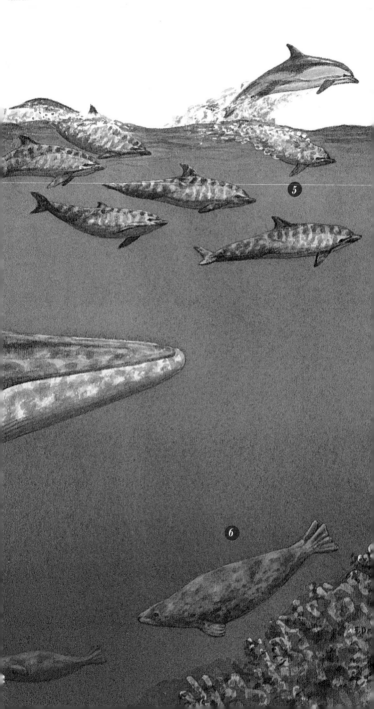

● Dolphins can more easily be seen from the shore, even if certain species or populations are distinctly pelagic. Also, they are more gregarious than the large cetaceans and may gather in very large groups.

● Some species associate naturally and may occasionally be seen together. For example, striped and common dolphin may be seen hunting food in the same area, attracted by shoals of fish.

The Coast

The sea is more varied as a habitat than it appears to be. This is even more true near the coast where the proximity of the land, the nature of the shoreline and pressure from man have an influence on marine life. Animals are occasionally washed up on the shore by the sea.

● Where there are many people, marine species usually keep away. Sparsely populated areas are best for making sightings.

Some species of seal like a well-sheltered sandy inlet where they can bask and give birth to their young

A headland jutting out to sea has an effect on currents locally and therefore on fish and plankton movement.

● High cliffs are good vantage points for looking out to sea.

● The slope of the sea-bed influences the establishment of wildlife: as depth increases, so light diminishes and seaweed and plant plankton disappear.

Marine mammals use the reef on which the lighthouse is built as a landmark

● Among marine mammals, it is **seals** which are the most common at the coast. At low tide when the beach itself is too crowded with people, they like resting on islands. From these sites, the animals can get back into the water quickly.

● **Sand banks** just showing on the surface of the water or appearing at low tide are sought after as basking places by common seals. On the other hand, species adapted for life in deep water, such as sperm whales and the large cetaceans, avoid them.

The salinity of seawater is affected by the presence of a river or estuary: these areas, which are rich in fish or various other forms of food, may attract marine mammals

● The shore separates and links the terrestrial and marine worlds. The sea is a three-dimensional habitat: marine mammals are well adapted to it and can exploit the different resources available between the surface and the deep water.

● The submarine 'landscape' includes peaks, mountains, gorges, lowlands, well sheltered or more open valleys. These sites and the resources they offer are fully known by the species inhabiting an area. So, in order to understand the distribution of marine mammals better, it can be useful to study underwater maps.

Anatomy

The overall shape (and therefore the entire anatomy) of marine mammals is very much determined by where they live. The most remarkable adaption occurs among the cetaceans whose streamlined shape for a long time led people to think they were fish. However, they are definitely mammals.

Arched jaw characteristic of whalebone whales: the baleen plates (or whalebone) which are fixed to the upper jaw develop in the space between the jaws

Minke whale skull

● Whalebone whales feed by filtering plankton, although some also catch small fish living in close shoals. The diet of toothed cetaceans and seals is very different.

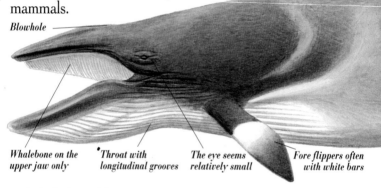

Blowhole

Whalebone on the upper jaw only

Throat with longitudinal grooves

The eye seems relatively small

Fore flippers often with white bars

● The body shape of the **minke whale** (above) is typical of the cetaceans.

● The **grey seal,** like other pinnipeds, looks more like a cetacean than a terrestrial mammal.

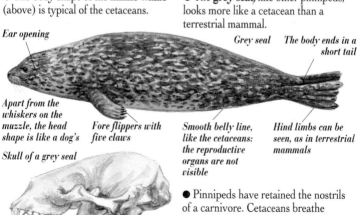

Ear opening

Grey seal

The body ends in a short tail

Apart from the whiskers on the muzzle, the head shape is like a dog's

Fore flippers with five claws

Smooth belly line, like the cetaceans: the reproductive organs are not visible

Hind limbs can be seen, as in terrestrial mammals

Skull of a grey seal

The teeth of a seal are all the same, unlike those of terrestrial carnivores

● Pinnipeds have retained the nostrils of a carnivore. Cetaceans breathe through a blowhole on top of the head. In the case of toothed whales, there is one hole, while whalebone whales have two. Their respiratory tract is completely separate from their mouth.

# of Marine Mammals

Shark

Dolphin

● It is easy to distinguish between a dolphin and a shark on the surface: the latter has a vertical tail fin which projects out of the water behind the dorsal fin. Also, the dolphin has to lift the blowhole on top of its head clear of the water in order to breathe, but the shark does not have a blowhole.

Small dorsal fin at the tail end of the body

● The **tail** of a **whale** (everything behind the dorsal fin) is used for propulsion: it is therefore very muscular.

Broad, distinctly forked, flukes

● A **bottle-nosed dolphin skeleton** shows the development of the hand and the near absence of the pelvic girdle. The cervical vertebrae are usually fused.

The spinal column gives firm support for the muscles used in swimming

The bones of the hand have evolved into flippers

Numerous conical teeth, all alike

● Unlike the seals, whales have no hair.

Dolphins have a beak but porpoises do not (see p16)

Common dolphin

The dorsal fin is often very pronounced

Colours vary between species and may be strongly contrasting

Flukes

● Comparatively speaking, **dolphins** have a smaller head and shorter body than whales.

● As with all the cetaceans, all visible traces of hind limbs have disappeared.

9

Common Seal

The common seal, one of the smaller seals, can be found all around the shores of the North Sea and North Atlantic. It has started breeding again on the Channel coast in France, after being practically eliminated by fishermen in the middle years of this century.

In August, the males leap out of the water in front of the females, partly to impress them and partly to see off any possible competitors

● When the tide is coming in, **common seals** raise their heads and hind flippers, adopting a banana-like position, to keep themselves out of the water.

● Common seals eat crustaceans and fish. The young feed partly on shrimps while an adult animal chooses flat fish or mullet.

Grey seal: in front view, the nostrils are almost parallel

Common seal: in front view, the nostrils form a V

● When in the water, the **common seal** bobs up and down, regularly poking its head out, then diving again, often to fish.

Mark made by the belly　　*Flipper marks*

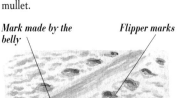

● The common seal drags itself over the sand using its two fore flippers simultaneously and leaving a characteristic track behind.

Male grey seal: the nose continues the line of the forehead

Common seal: muzzle pronounced as in dogs

● As seals turn over from one side to the other, they look two-coloured, with one dry side and one wet side.

Common seals will bask in the sun at low tide if they are undisturbed

The gull has come to feed on the droppings or placenta left by the mother

● The common seal, which prefers sandy beaches that are exposed at low tide or sand banks cut off by the sea, will use rocky shores if the rocks are covered in seaweed.

● In June, the females give birth to a pup: it has to be able to swim a few hours later at the first high tide.

Weight: from 80 or 100kg up to 150kg for the heaviest. Males are larger than females.

● The black-flecked coat has colour tones ranging from grey brown to yellow. The appearance of the **common seal** is often altered by the light, and the fact that its coat may be wet or dry.

Length of an adult common seal: from about 1.2 to 2m

Grey Seal

Males fight to win a section of the beach where they will establish a harem once the females arrive

The grey sea lives in the North Atlantic. Its population is centred around the British Isles, the Scottish coasts in particular. France, with a few colonies in Brittany, forms the southern limit of its distribution in Europe. It is one of the largest seals in our area.

● Often the first glimpse of a seal is a head raised out of the water before the animal makes another dive. It is not always easy to make an identification.

● The **grey seal** eats mainly crabs, shrimps, cod and salmon, though its diet varies from region to region.

Seals may behave like a cork in the water: they rest in a vertical position, putting their heads out of the water from time to time in order to breathe

Male: characteristic straight profile, the nose an extension of the forehead

In side view, the profile of the females and young can be confused with that of the common seal

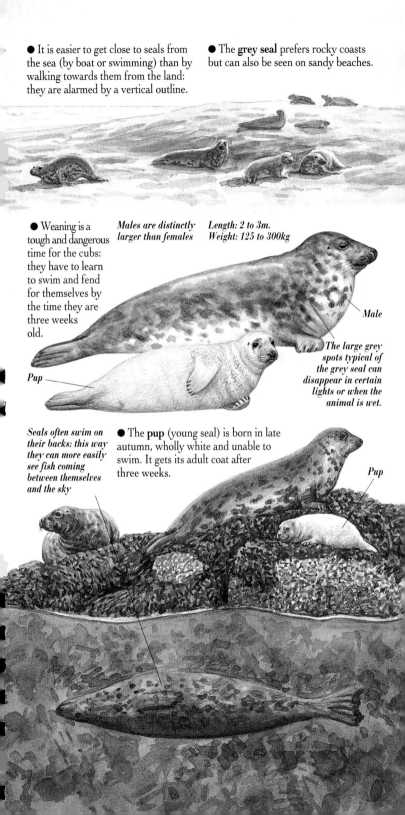

● It is easier to get close to seals from the sea (by boat or swimming) than by walking towards them from the land: they are alarmed by a vertical outline.

● The **grey seal** prefers rocky coasts but can also be seen on sandy beaches.

● Weaning is a tough and dangerous time for the cubs: they have to learn to swim and fend for themselves by the time they are three weeks old.

Males are distinctly larger than females

Length: 2 to 3m. Weight: 125 to 300kg

Male

Pup

The large grey spots typical of the grey seal can disappear in certain lights or when the animal is wet.

Seals often swim on their backs: this way they can more easily see fish coming between themselves and the sky

● The **pup** (young seal) is born in late autumn, wholly white and unable to swim. It gets its adult coat after three weeks.

Pup

Monk Seal, Walrus

Few people have any idea that there are seals in the Mediterranean. This is, however, the case but not, perhaps, for much longer: the monk seal is the most threatened of the marine mammals. The world today leaves it no room on the shores that it has occupied for thousands of years. The last remaining individuals inhabit the Aegean Sea. The other five pinnipeds discussed here are all Arctic species: they only rarely come south, as far as the English Channel.

● The **monk seal** breeds on beaches: nowadays, it is driven off by boats and holidaymakers.

Monk seal
Length: up to 3m
Weight: 300kg

Dark chestnut brown, often with a lighter patch on the belly

Bearded seal
Length: 2.40m. Weight: 200 to 250kg.

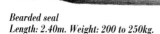

● The **bearded seal**, is more solitary than the other species. It can be recognised by its long moustache-like whiskers, large size and square hind flippers.

Ringed seal: it owes its name to the pattern on its coat.
Length: 1.30m
Weight: up to 100kg

● **Ringed seals**, the smallest of the seals, are relatively numerous around the Arctic. They are eaten by Eskimos and polar bears.

Walrus
Length: 3m
Weight: 1300kg

● The very thick skin and blubber of the walrus is a protection against the cold of the polar seas. It feeds on shellfish and fish on the sea bed.

and Accidental Seals

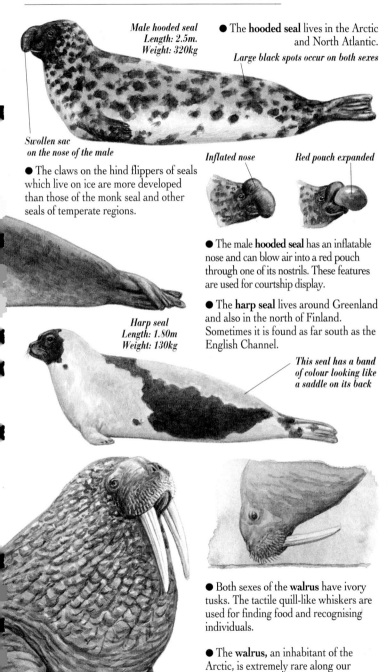

Male hooded seal
Length: 2.5m.
Weight: 320kg

● The **hooded seal** lives in the Arctic and North Atlantic.

Large black spots occur on both sexes

Swollen sac on the nose of the male

● The claws on the hind flippers of seals which live on ice are more developed than those of the monk seal and other seals of temperate regions.

Inflated nose   *Red pouch expanded*

● The male **hooded seal** has an inflatable nose and can blow air into a red pouch through one of its nostrils. These features are used for courtship display.

● The **harp seal** lives around Greenland and also in the north of Finland. Sometimes it is found as far south as the English Channel.

Harp seal
Length: 1.80m
Weight: 130kg

This seal has a band of colour looking like a saddle on its back

● Both sexes of the **walrus** have ivory tusks. The tactile quill-like whiskers are used for finding food and recognising individuals.

● The **walrus,** an inhabitant of the Arctic, is extremely rare along our coasts. It lives in colonies, only stray individuals ever being found in northern Europe.

15

Porpoises and Killer Whales

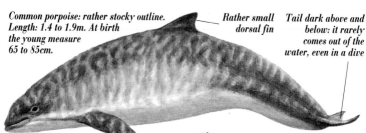

Common porpoise: rather stocky outline. Length: 1.4 to 1.9m. At birth the young measure 65 to 85cm.

Rather small dorsal fin

Tail dark above and below: it rarely comes out of the water, even in a dive

Porpoises are often confused with dolphins but belong to a different family, the Phocaenidae. They are difficult to approach or study as they are extremely timid. They like to frequent coastal regions but populations near our shores are decreasing as they are adversely affected by water pollution.

● The **common porpoise** is one of the smallest cetaceans known, occurring in the Black Sea, the Mediterranean Sea, the Atlantic and the North Sea. It appears to make seasonal migrations, sometimes coming up rivers.

Killer whale (Orca) Length: 4.5 to more than 9m

● **Porpoises** are often sighted in small groups but rarely come close to boats. They move very rapidly when hunting. In calm seas, they can be seen resting, the top of their head and forward part of the back just breaking the surface of the water.

Male narwhal

● Stranded **porpoises** are often sick or weak individuals. Finding a porpoise on the beach that has been drowned in a fishing net, is unfortunately too frequent.

● The **porpoise**, an animal of shallow waters, frequenting estuaries and rivers, is exposed to many dangers.

A porpoise caught in a net and stranded

Rather small dorsal fin

Rather long snout

False killer whale
Length: 4 to 6m

Angled pectoral fin

● The **false killer whale** is a large, almost entirely black dolphin, with a very rounded body shape, mostly encountered at sea.

Male killer whale

Tall triangular dorsal fin

Light band behind the dorsal fin

● The **killer whale** is the largest of the dolphins. The male is distinctly larger than the female, the dorsal fin reaching 2m in the oldest and dominant individuals. The black and white colouring acts like camouflage, an important asset to this predator. It is present in all seas.

Tail black above and white beneath

The white patch on its flank breaks the outline of the whale so it is not seen by its prey

Length: 4 to 5m

Flukes with characteristically rounded end

Flipper turned up at the tip and slightly rimmed

● The white whale (beluga) and narwhal lack a dorsal fin.

It is impossible to mistake the narwhal because of its shape and particularly the long tusk sported by the males. This species rarely leaves the Arctic coastal waters.

Only the males have this continually-growing tusk. Its use seems to be restricted to fighting between males.

The white whale is an Arctic species. In Europe, it occurs along the northern coastline of Norway.

Length: 3 to 5m

The adult white whale is entirely white (at birth, grey-brown)

No dorsal fin

Prominent broadly rounded forehead (melon)

Bottle-nosed Dolphins

Many shades of bluish-grey

Bottle-nosed dolphin: adult males reach 4m

Very visible, slightly hooked dorsal fin

● Deep sea **bottle-nosed dolphins** are lighter coloured and heavier than those which live near the coast.

Belly lighter in colour than the sides and back

● The **bottle-nosed dolphin's** famous smile is explained by the position of its facial muscles and tissues.

It may not be the best known, but the bottle-nosed dolphin is the most popular, thanks to being seen on film and television screens and in aquariums. It inhabits most of the world's oceans, only avoiding the coldest waters. Tropical forms are smaller than ours: size and volume are an advantage in the struggle against the cold.

● **Bottle-nosed dolphins** live in shoals that are sometimes large, with perhaps several dozen individuals. When danger threatens, perhaps in the form of a shark, the shoal acts as one and the young swim very close to their mothers.

● Dolphins like boats, partly because they are curious, but also because they can take advantage of the bow-wave. Some individuals will allow people to come close to them but it is not known why.

● When the sea is rough and during the night, dolphins find their way by echolocation.

● The young are very playful, seeming to take pleasure in leaping out of the water while the adults swim around or rest in the water.

● Leaps may also be a sign of tension or agitation.

● The young come into the world tail first so as to delay for as long as

possible the first intake of breath. As soon as the baby is born, the mother pushes it to the surface to breathe.

A new-born dolphin is 1m long

Group of bottle-nosed dolphins

This hollow is occupied by part of the echo location system.

Conical teeth, all alike: 40 to 50 on each jaw

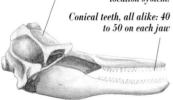

● The skull of the **bottle-nosed dolphin** is typical of the dolphins.

● It is difficult to assess the size of a group as not all the dolphins surface at the same time. The apparent synchronisation of their movements is deceptive.

● **Bottle-nosed dolphins** hunt in groups for fish.

Common and Striped

The common dolphin is found in nearly all of the world's seas, in temperate water between 10° and 28°C. It is an active animal, living in groups ranging from a few individuals to several hundred and often swimming alongside ships. The common and striped dolphin are occasionally seen together in their   fishing grounds.

● The **striped dolphin**, which is common in the Mediterranean, was painted on the ancient frescoes in the palace of Knossos in Crete.

Small rather pointed dorsal fin

Common dolphin: Length: 1.7 to 2.4m

Long beak

Dark triangle on the back behind the dorsal fin

Pale grey patch on the rear flank

Yellow patch on the forward flank

Dolphins

Skull of the common dolphin: 80 to 120 small pointed conical teeth on each jaw

Striped dolphin

Light blue-grey flash reaching back towards the dorsal fin

Common dolphin

Two diamond-shaped patches on the flank: one grey, the other yellow

● The two species can be separated by the characteristic colours on their flanks.

● The **striped dolphin** is more common around boats in the Atlantic and Mediterranean than elsewhere. It leaps and performs spectacular acrobatic feats. A viral infection killed thousands in the Mediterranean between 1990 and 1992, at a time when it had become very numerous in that area.

● **Common dolphin, striped dolphin** and **tunny fish** hunt the same small fish in some areas, where also fishing boats are also found in large numbers. Their seine nets cannot distinguish between tunny and dolphin.

Rather large sickle-shaped dorsal fin

Flanks distinctly bluish grey

Very pronounced beak

Rather slender, scarcely forked flukes

*Striped dolphin
Length: 1.8 to 2.5m*

Pilot Whale

Characteristic black colour

The white patch on the throat is sometimes visible

The black long-finned pilot whale is a huge dolphin. Its large rounded head is characteristic, as is its strongly gregarious instinct which sometimes causes large-scale strandings. In the northern hemisphere, it frequents the temperate waters of the Atlantic from Iceland to the Canaries.

● The **pilot whale** is curious, holding its head out of water to look at a boat.

Long-finned pilot whale

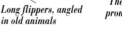

Large rounded head: the end of the melon extends beyond the point of the mouth

Dorsal fin very pronounced but distinctly rounded. The hook is most pronounced in the males.

● During the day, **pilot whales** often rest near the surface and are quite easy to watch. Sometimes they sleep lying on one side clearly leaving a flipper and one of the tail flukes out of the water.

Long flippers, angled in old animals

● The pattern on the belly of the **black pilot whale** is characteristic but difficult to see unless the animal is stranded. The white varies in prominence from one individual to another.

Cuttlefish

● In the Faroe Islands, north of Scotland, late summer is the time for hunting the pilot whales: nowadays this tradition is hard to justify.

● **Pilot whales** feed on cephalopods, particularly squid.

● The fishing grounds, which attract sea birds and cetaceans, often present an amazing spectacle. Pilot whales feed during the night when the squid come to the surface but may also dive to a depth of 600m.

Skull of a pilot whale

Each jaw has between 16 and 24 teeth. The skull is massive.

● The **Risso's dolphin** or **grampus** is mainly pelagic. It may be seen in the English Channel, for example, when it comes close to the coast to feed on cuttlefish.

Risso's dolphin
Length: 4 to 6m

The body is grey and appears to be entirely covered with white streaks

White belly and a yellow streak on the hind part of the flank

White-sided dolphin
Length 2.5m

White-beaked dolphin
Length: 2.5 to 3m

Light grey patch on back of dorsal fin

White beak

White line on the flank

White-beaked dolphin: white patch just above the tail

White-sided dolphin: yellow streak on the flanks near the tail

● The **white-beaked dolphin** and **white-sided dolphin**, which both inhabit the north Atlantic, are deep sea animals, rarely approaching the coast and not easy to tell apart.

Sperm Whale

The sperm whale is the largest toothed cetacean and also one of the most amazing. Its silhouette is quite unique, with the head occupying one third of the total length of the body! It occurs in every sea in the world, only avoiding shallow waters (less than 200m deep).

Sperm whale

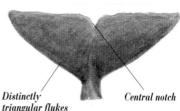

Distinctly triangular flukes

Central notch

● The **massive square head** of the sperm whale is characteristic. The head of the male is even larger than that of the female. The spermaceti tissue contained within the rounded snout allows the animal to dive to great depths.

Blowhole

Head sometimes with lighter areas

Slender jaw, hidden away under the head

Eye

Short heavy flippers. The body is primarily grey. The skin has a creased appearance.

Length: 11 to 12m (females), 15 to 18m (males)

40 to 50 conical teeth, all on the lower jaw, each weighing up to 1kg

● **Sperm whales** live in schools of females and young that are sometimes very large. Males join them at breeding time. The females rarely go beyond latitude 40° north or south while the males go as far as the ice fields.

The dorsal fin is replaced by one or more humps

Sperm whale skull

● The spermaceti oil is located above and in front of the jaw: by means of this substance, the sperm whale is able to control its density when diving deeply.

Diving record of the sperm whale: 3000m

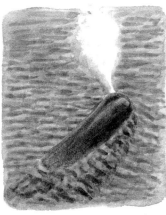

● The **spout of the sperm whale** is easy to recognise: it is a single spout, pointing forward and to the left of the animal.

● **Sperm whales** feed primarily on squid which they catch in deep water.

● When the **sperm whale** dives, the tail is held vertically before disappearing. The whale can remain under water for more than an hour and dive to a depth of over 2000m.

Voluminous melon overhanging the beak

Bottle-nosed whale

Grey-black in colour, lighter on the belly
Length: up to 9m

● The three toothed whales on the right are little known because they are shy and live in deep water. They do not leap out of the water and are difficult to study, unless stranded.

The bottle-nosed whale lives in the deep waters of the north Atlantic.

Cuvier's beaked whale

Cuvier's beaked whale, with a head like the beak of a goose, avoids only polar waters.

Light colour, massive silhouette
Length: up to 7m

Sowerby's whale

Length: 5 to 7m

Sowerby's whale, together with a dozen or so closely related species, inhabits the deep seas of the world, feeding mainly on squid. All are little known.

● These beaked whales sometimes have only one or two pairs of teeth on the lower jaw.

25

Rorquals

The fin whale (common rorqual or razorback), the second largest of the whales, is the most streamlined, slender and rapid of the rorquals. It occurs in the seas all around Europe, including the western part of the Mediterranean.

● **Fin whale** feeding. In a boat, it is possible to get close to small schools. But they are unpredictable and could move off in any direction.

Fin whale
Length: 15 to 23m

Well developed dorsal fin

Sei whale

● The **fin whale** can reach 30km per hour.

● **Fin whales** eat shrimps and small fish swimming in a shoal. The **minke whale** ignores the shrimps and swallows much bigger prey than the larger species of rorqual.

● Each kind of rorqual catches different prey, so reducing competition between the species.

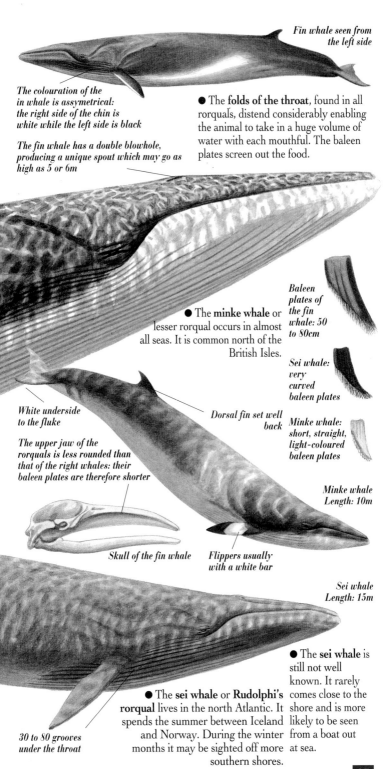

Fin whale seen from the left side

The colouration of the in whale is assymetrical: the right side of the chin is white while the left side is black

The fin whale has a double blowhole, producing a unique spout which may go as high as 5 or 6m

● The **folds of the throat**, found in all rorquals, distend considerably enabling the animal to take in a huge volume of water with each mouthful. The baleen plates screen out the food.

Baleen plates of the fin whale: 50 to 80cm

● The **minke whale** or lesser rorqual occurs in almost all seas. It is common north of the British Isles.

Sei whale: very curved baleen plates

White underside to the fluke

The upper jaw of the rorquals is less rounded than that of the right whales: their baleen plates are therefore shorter

Dorsal fin set well back

Minke whale: short, straight, light-coloured baleen plates

Minke whale Length: 10m

Skull of the fin whale

Flippers usually with a white bar

Sei whale Length: 15m

● The **sei whale** or **Rudolphi's rorqual** lives in the north Atlantic. It spends the summer between Iceland and Norway. During the winter months it may be sighted off more southern shores.

● The **sei whale** is still not well known. It rarely comes close to the shore and is more likely to be seen from a boat out at sea.

30 to 80 grooves under the throat

27

Blue, Right

The blue whale, or Sibbald's rorqual, shares the same sad fate as the right and humpback whales: hunting has brought these three species to the point of extinction. At the present time, populations of the right and particularly of the humpback whales are showing clear signs of recovery. This is really not the case with the blue whales: it would appear that hunting has continued illegally despite official protection.

Spout of a humpback whale: rather broad, 2 or 3m high

Dive: hump visible

Spout of a right whale: double, V-shaped, up to 5m high

Dive: no dorsal fin

Spout of a blue whale: up to 10m high, the highest of all

Dive: dorsal fin not very conspicuous

● Whalers in times gone by were expert at recognising whales by their spout: the size, shape and timing are characteristic.

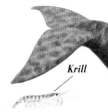

Krill

● The blue whale and the right whale feed solely on krill while the humpback also takes fish.

● The **blue whale** is the largest animal in the world: more than 20m long (the record is 33m), with the mass estimated at up to 190 tonnes.

● Whalebone whales each have a characteristic kind of baleen plate. These can really only be studied on stranded animals.

Baleen plate of the blue whale

Baleen plate of the right whale: 1–2m

Baleen plate of the humpback whale

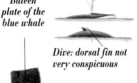

Seen from above, the blue whale's head is U-shaped, while the other rorquals have a narrower, V-shaped snout

60–90 very distendable folds on the throat

Long slender flippers

The throat folds extend as far as the navel

and Humpback Whales

Flukes of the humpback whale. Each individual has a unique pattern under the flukes.

The right whale holds its tail erect when diving

No dorsal fin

The underside of the flukes of the blue whale is uniformly blue. The tail does not come up when the animal dives.

● When whales dive, some of them bring their tail out of the water. Species, even individuals, can be identified by the tail.

Huge head, with a swollen area (the bonnet) on the snout

Dark colouration, a few white patches on the belly

Square flippers

● The **right whale** has almost disappeared from our waters. It differs greatly in shape from the other whales.

Small dorsal fin on an irregular swelling

Flippers: 3 to 5m long. These are the longest flippers among whales

Flippers with white patches

Dorsal fin inconspicuous

● The **humpback whale** is known for the spectacular leaps it performs in its breeding grounds. Tropical seas are the the best places to observe this (for example, the Antilles, California and Hawaii).

Very broad flukes (up to 5m across)

● The **blue whale** is so-called because of its bluish colour. Once cosmopolitan, occurring in all the seas of the world, it is distinctly rare today. The mouth of the St Lawrence, in Canada, is a well-known place for watching them.

Very heavily built, muscular tail

29

● Around the British Isles, the otter can be seen going among seals basking at low tide.

Otter

Bladder wrack

Grey seal

● The **otter** conceals itself and fishes in the bladder wrack which is plentiful on the shores where it lives.

● **Otters** are active night and day, and at both high and low tide. It is therefore difficult to anticipate and watch its comings and goings.

● **Otters** feed on fish and are especially fond of eels which are common in patches of seaweed.

The otter mainly inhabits lakes and rivers but there are populations on the coast which fish in the sea. Most occur in mainland Scotland and the neighbouring islands: the Hebrides, Orkneys and Shetlands.

● It is not easy to find **otter tracks** on the sand or seaweed. Signs of their presence can be found just inland, where there is water: otters need fresh water to wash the salt out of their fur so that it stays waterproof.

Male: 1 to 1.4m (including tail) and 10 to 15kg
Female: 0.9 to 1.1m (including tail) and 6 to 12kg.

When standing, it uses its powerful tail as a support

Hindquarters higher than shoulders

Light-coloured throat

Almost invisible when swimming: only the head projects, leaving a wake

Track: pads on the feet do not always show

Stiff whiskers

Although the seals and whales have descended from terrestrial ancestors, and still retain air-breathing lungs, they are all beautifully adapted for life in the sea. But their bodes have become adapted for marine life in very different ways. The seals have retained all four legs, although they have been converted into flippers, but the whales have lost all trace of their back legs. Seals all come ashore to breed, but whales spend their entire lives in the water and are completely helpless if washed up on the shore. The ways in which the animals have become adapted for marine life are briefly outlined on the following pages.

Classification

Seals and whales have very separate histories. The seals are close to terrestrial carnivores while whales and dolphins are closer to distant relations of the hoofed mammals who took to the seas about 60 million years ago. The two living groups of whales (toothed and whalebone whales) were preceded by a group which has disappeared leaving no representative behind.

Hapalodectes
(~53 million years ago)

● The transition from terrestrial ancestor to cetacean occurred over a long period of time, the fore legs gradually becoming flippers, the hind legs disappearing and the blowhole appearing.

Ganges dolphin

● The **Platanistidae** contains five species of small cetaceans, only one of which is marine. The others live in the warm waters of the Amazon, Indus, Ganges and Yangtze rivers and are called river dolphins.

● Three suborders of Cetacea are recognised.
- the **Archaeoceti** are now extinct.
- the **Odontoceti,** toothed whales, comprising seven families.
- the **Mysticeti,** whalebone whales with baleen plates, comprising four families.

There are 78 species of cetacean living today, many of which are still little known. Their genealogical table can be drawn up but the links between the various branches is not understood.

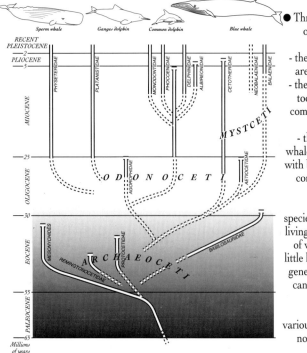

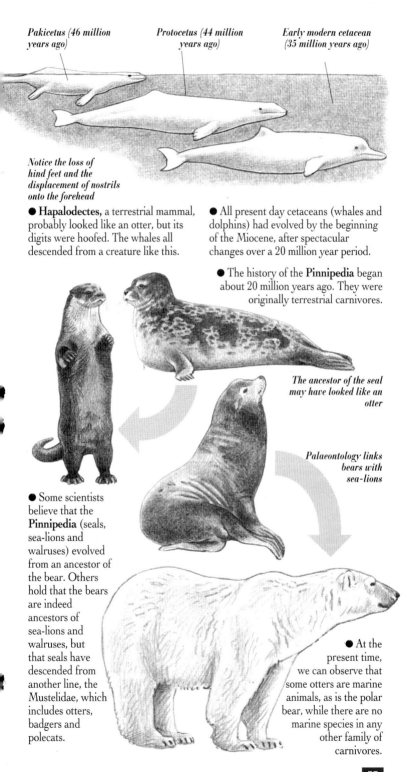

Pakicetus (46 million years ago)

Protocetus (44 million years ago)

Early modern cetacean (35 million years ago)

Notice the loss of hind feet and the displacement of nostrils onto the forehead

● **Hapalodectes,** a terrestrial mammal, probably looked like an otter, but its digits were hoofed. The whales all descended from a creature like this.

● All present day cetaceans (whales and dolphins) had evolved by the beginning of the Miocene, after spectacular changes over a 20 million year period.

● The history of the **Pinnipedia** began about 20 million years ago. They were originally terrestrial carnivores.

The ancestor of the seal may have looked like an otter

Palaeontology links bears with sea-lions

● Some scientists believe that the **Pinnipedia** (seals, sea-lions and walruses) evolved from an ancestor of the bear. Others hold that the bears are indeed ancestors of sea-lions and walruses, but that seals have descended from another line, the Mustelidae, which includes otters, badgers and polecats.

● At the present time, we can observe that some otters are marine animals, as is the polar bear, while there are no marine species in any other family of carnivores.

Adaptation to the Sea

Pinnipedia (seals) and
Cetacea (whales) are
outstanding on account of
their adapation to the marine
environment. However, the
anatomical solutions to the
basic problems of
locomotion, respiration and
heat conservation are not the
same in these two groups of
marine mammals.

*Cetacean skin: thick
layer of sub-
cutaneous blubber
(up to 50cm in large
species), no hair*

*Pinniped skin: a
combination of fur
and subcutaneous
blubber. The moult
is an important time
in the animal's year.*

*Terrestrial
mammal's skin, less
effective in cold
water: less fat, fur
not so thick*

● Marine mammals breath in air,
Pinnipedia through nostrils and Cetacea
through a blowhole (see p8). They can
all remain under water for a long time
(see figure, p39), but come up at regular
intervals to breathe: when whales
breathe out, they expel their powerful
spout.

● The skin of cetaceans covers a thick layer
of blubber which encloses the body. This
blubber conserves heat and absorbs
turbulences created by the swimming
motion. The body surface forms hollows
where turbulence develops and eliminates it
so that the animal can move more efficiently
through the water.

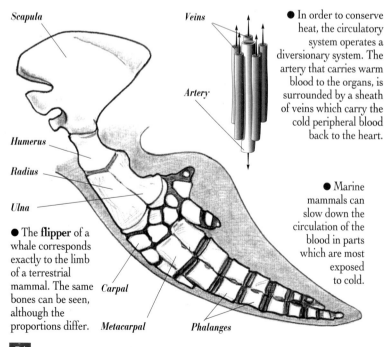

Scapula

Veins

Artery

● In order to conserve
heat, the circulatory
system operates a
diversionary system. The
artery that carries warm
blood to the organs, is
surrounded by a sheath
of veins which carry the
cold peripheral blood
back to the heart.

Humerus

Radius

Ulna

● The **flipper** of a
whale corresponds
exactly to the limb
of a terrestrial
mammal. The same
bones can be seen,
although the
proportions differ.

Carpal

Metacarpal

Phalanges

● Marine
mammals can
slow down the
circulation of the
blood in parts
which are most
exposed
to cold.

● To improve the streamlining of their body, marine mammals have only the bare minimum of protuberances on the outside, making it difficult to distinguish between males and females. To do this, openings on the belly must be counted and, in particular, their relative positions must be observed.

● Males are larger than females, apart from the rorquals, where the opposite applies.

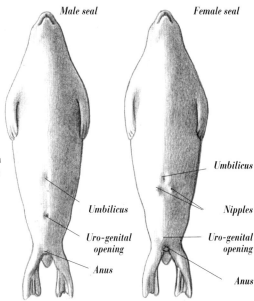

Male seal

Female seal

Umbilicus

Umbilicus

Nipples

Uro-genital opening

Uro-genital opening

Anus

Anus

● Monk and bearded seals have four nipples while other European species have only two. Among cetaceans, the nipples are hidden deep in a furrow: the female releases milk under pressure from the calf's mouth.

● To swim, cetaceans move their tail up and down and seals sway their body from side to side. Sea-lions and fur seals flap their front flippers like wings to push them through the water.

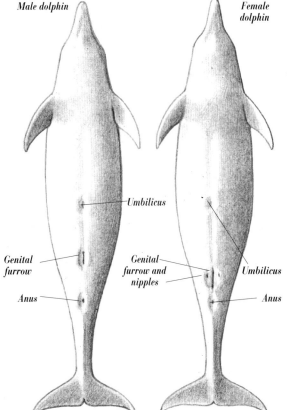

Male dolphin

Female dolphin

Umbilicus

Genital furrow

Genital furrow and nipples

Umbilicus

Anus

Anus

Migration

Cetacean and bird migrations are among the most spectacular. In the summer, species journey to polar regions in search of food, returning in winter to tropical waters for the breeding season. Migrations therefore occur in opposite directions in the two hemispheres.

● Several schools of **pilot whales** gather in any one breeding area. This is why, in a school, the males are not necessarily the fathers of the calves.

● In our area, the pinnipeds do not migrate but, in the southern hemisphere, some species of sea-lion and seal do make seasonal journeys, coming ashore only for breeding.

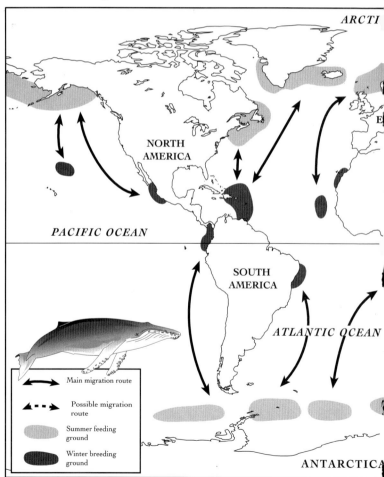

ARCTI

NORTH
AMERICA

E

PACIFIC OCEAN

SOUTH
AMERICA

ATLANTIC OCEAN

Main migration route

Possible migration
route

Summer feeding
ground

Winter breeding
ground

ANTARCTICA

● Between their various activities, porpoises can rest and sleep with one eye open, or rather with one half of the brain active, so as to keep their breathing under control.

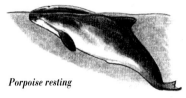

Porpoise resting

● Some species are territorial all year, or for part of the year. So it has been possible to study groups of resident bottle-nosed dolphin, such as those near Sein Island off the Brittany coast.

Resting area
Play area
Fishing ground

1 Km

Imaginary map showing approximate areas of dolphin activity

● In order to understand the pattern of dolphin activity, the areas where they live have been divided into squares so that their position and corresponding activity can be recorded. Their timetable is fairly predictable but of course varies with the state of the sea and the tides.

● We are beginning to have a better knowledge of the migrations of the **humpback whale** (see map). There are several populations in each hemisphere and exchanges between populations are infrequent. Individuals hardly ever cross the equator. For other species, the breeding grounds are known but not the feeding grounds, or vice versa.

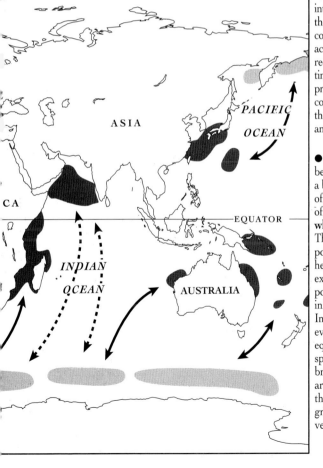

ASIA

PACIFIC OCEAN

CA

EQUATOR

INDIAN OCEAN

AUSTRALIA

Food

78 cetacean and 33 pinniped species inhabit the waters of the world. This wide range of marine mammals is possible because they vary greatly in size, distribution and diet.

● Toothed cetaceans (dolphins, porpoises, pilot whales, sperm whales) locate their prey by echolocation.

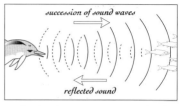

succession of sound waves

reflected sound

● The three major groups preyed on by marine mammals are pelagic crustaceans (species of shrimp known as krill), cephalopods (primarily squid) and fish.

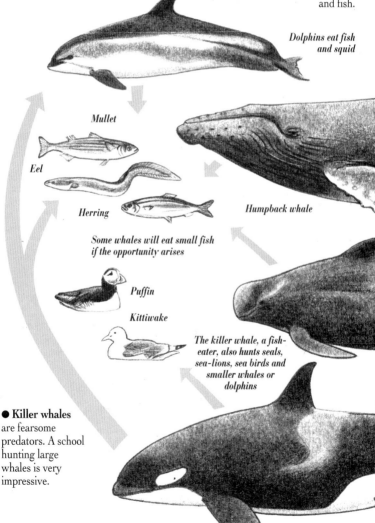

Dolphins eat fish and squid

Mullet

Eel

Herring

Humpback whale

Some whales will eat small fish if the opportunity arises

Puffin

Kittiwake

The killer whale, a fish-eater, also hunts seals, sea-lions, sea birds and smaller whales or dolphins

● **Killer whales** are fearsome predators. A school hunting large whales is very impressive.

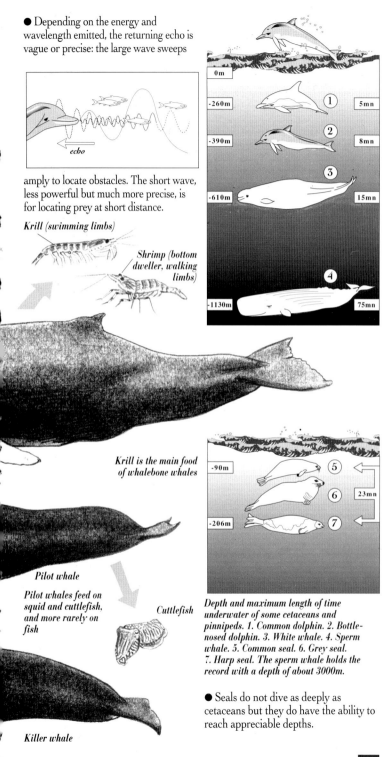

● Depending on the energy and wavelength emitted, the returning echo is vague or precise: the large wave sweeps

echo

amply to locate obstacles. The short wave, less powerful but much more precise, is for locating prey at short distance.

Krill (swimming limbs)

Shrimp (bottom dweller, walking limbs)

0m

-260m   ①   5mn

-390m   ②   8mn

③   15mn
-610m

④
-1130m   75mn

Krill is the main food of whalebone whales

-90m   ⑤

⑥   23mn
-206m   ⑦

Pilot whale

Pilot whales feed on squid and cuttlefish, and more rarely on fish

Cuttlefish

Depth and maximum length of time underwater of some cetaceans and pinnipeds. 1. Common dolphin. 2. Bottle-nosed dolphin. 3. White whale. 4. Sperm whale. 5. Common seal. 6. Grey seal. 7. Harp seal. The sperm whale holds the record with a depth of about 3000m.

● Seals do not dive as deeply as cetaceans but they do have the ability to reach appreciable depths.

Killer whale

39

Strandings

Strandings of whales and dolphins have always occurred locally. We cannot explain the large scale strandings of pilot whales or of those giants of the sea, the rorquals and sperm whales. One thing is certain: these are not suicides.

Paradoxically, strandings are a source of information: some species have only ever been seen as stranded specimens.

● The **monk seal** of the Mediterranean sums up the fate suffered by many marine mammals: direct destruction, pollution, overcrowding of the beaches by people, over-fishing, drift nets.

● The chance of saving a stranded dolphin are slight. Intervention in the case of the pinnipeds is more successful because they can live out of water. Several rescue centres specialise in the rescue of seal pups.

Dolphin caught in a drift net

● Every year, nets are the cause of death by drowning, not only of thousands of whales and dolphins, but also of pinnipeds, sea birds and sea turtles.

and Disease

● In 1989, 20,000 common seals died in the North Sea. In 1990 and 1991, thousands of striped dolphins died in the Mediterranean. The cause of these ecological catastrophes was two viruses, whose effect was reinforced by the pollution of our coastal waters.

● There are several causes for strandings. Whales may die out at sea and be cast up on the shore. Some animals get stranded by accident if they come too close to the shore, in bad weather, for example. In the case of collective strandings, the gregarious instinct may compel the whole group to become stranded if they are staying close to an immobilised individual calling for help. A sick dominant adult could call the rest of the group onto the beach.

● Sperm whale strandings are often the result of errors in navigation.

Sperm whale stranded on the coast of the English Channel (below). The slender lower jaw under the vast head is clearly visible.

Where and When to Watch

Cetaceans can be seen at almost any point in the sea but certain places and seasons are best for watching them. The tourist industry is developing sea trips which offer the public the opportunity to discover whales, birds and fish, and also the sea turtles which inhabit our shores. The limit to be set on these activities has still to be defined, so that these species can be seen without to much disturbance.

● The **loggerhead turtle** still breeds in the Mediterranean, around Greece and Turkey.

● The **leathery turtle**, the largest sea turtle, is regularly seen in the Pertuis Charentais in late summer. It feeds on jellyfish and sometimes suffocates after swallowing plastic bags in mistake for its prey.

● Fishermen and sailors often report interesting sites. Headlands are always good vantage points: marine mammals swim round them, hugging the coast.

● In temperate zones, late summer is a good time to watch species before they depart for warmer waters where they will spend the winter.

● A few world-renowned vantage points.

ARCTIC OCEAN

Disko Islands (Greenland) · Lofoten Islands · Hofn (Norway) · The Hebrides (Iceland) · Churchill (Canada) · Newfoundland (Canada) · West Coast of Ireland · The Hebrides (Scotland) · Glacier Bay (Alaska) · Vancouver Island (Canada) · Gulf of St Lawrence (Canada) · Azores (Portugal) · EUROPE · NORTH AMERICA · New England (USA) · California (USA) · Gulf of California (Mexico) · Bahamas (Mexico) · Gibraltar (United Kingdom) · Canary Islands (Spain) · ASIA · PACIFIC OCEAN · Shikoku Islands (Japan) · Ogasawara (Japan) · Hawaii (USA) · AFRICA · Trincomalee (Sri Lanka) · PACIFIC OCEAN · SOUTH AMERICA · ATLANTIC OCEAN · INDIAN OCEAN · Monkey Mia (Australia) · AUSTRALIA · Hervey Bay (Australia) · Hermanus (South Africa) · Valdès (Argentina) · Logan's Beach (Australia) · Kaikoura (New Zealand)

- *California (USA) and Baja California (Mexico) winter months until April (grey whale, sea-lion, seal, otter)- Antilles (humpback whale)*

- *Gulf of St Lawrence (Canada) late summer (cetaceans)*

- *Valdes Peninsula (Argentina) during the southern summer*

- *New Zealand*
- *Sri Lanka*

● Good binoculars (eg 10x40) are very useful. Avoid binoculars that are too heavy, especially for use in a boat.

● A **camera** with telephoto lens (200mm, for example) will capture often fleeting glimpses.

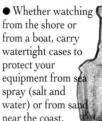

● Safety regulations must be obeyed on a boat. These include the wearing of a life jacket, particularly on small boats.

● Whether watching from the shore or from a boat, carry watertight cases to protect your equipment from sea spray (salt and water) or from sand near the coast.

1. Lofoten Islands, Norway: cetaceans, seals
2. Lake Ladoga, Russia: ringed seal
3. Gulf of Bothnia: grey and ringed seals
4. Hofn, Iceland: seals
5. Shetland and Orkney Islands, Scotland and
6. The Hebrides, Scotland: cetaceans, common and grey seals, otter

7. West coast, Scotland: porpoise, bottle-nosed dolphin, common and grey seals, otter
8. West coast, Ireland: cetaceans, common and grey seals
9. The Wash, England: common and grey seals
10. Wadden Sea: common and grey seals
11. Baie de la Somme, France: common and grey seals

12. Baie du Mont St Michel: common seal, bottle-nosed dolphin, Risso's dolphin
13. Molene, Sein and Ouessant Islands: bottle-nosed dolphin, grey seal
14. Pertuis Charentais: leathery turtle
15. Bassin d'Arcachon: bottle-nosed dolphin
16. Straits of Gibraltar: cetaceans

17. Gulf of Genoa, between Corsica and the French coast: cetaceans
18. Dalmatian coast: bottle-nosed dolphin
19. Ionian Sea, Greece: bottle-nosed dolphin, monk seal, loggerhead turtle,
20. Aegean Sea, Greece: dolphin, monk seal
21. Black Sea: common dolphin, porpoise
22. Dalyan, Turkey: loggerhead turtle

● A few renowned vantage points in Europe.

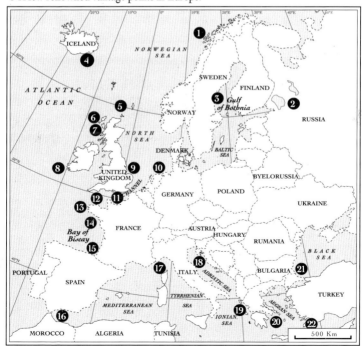

Threats and Protection

Divers free dolphins from a net

Logo of the International Whaling Commission which has fixed the quota for catching whales since 1946

All the large whales and numerous pinnipeds are threatened with the same fate as that suffered by the monk seal in the Antilles – extinction. Numerous societies, with the assistance of recognised scientists, are attempting to change attitudes and laws in respect of marine mammals.

● The **Mediterranean monk seal**, driven from the beaches by development and from the sea by excessive fishing, is threatened with extinction in the near future.

● Modern methods of large scale deep-sea fishing kill tens of thousands of dolphins every year. However, it is possible to help dolphins escape from the seine nets used for catching tunny.

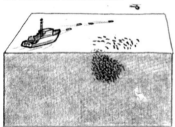

1. Once the tunny are found, small boats form a ring around them, carrying the net

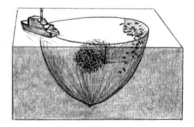

3. The panic-stricken dolphin get caught in the mesh and die from drowning

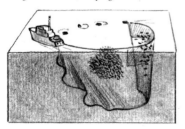

2. The huge net is deployed over a wide perimeter, forming a wall

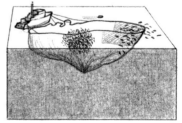

4. With one small boat, the dolphin could be guided out of the trap

44

● In spite of having only primitive equipment, the old whalers' actions have completely eliminated the Atlantic grey whale and almost exterminated the right whale.

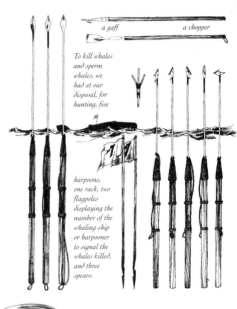

a gaff   a chopper

To kill whales and sperm whales, we had at our disposal, for hunting, five harpoons, one rack, two flagpoles displaying the number of the whaling ship or harpooner to signal the whales killed, and three spears.

● Aquariums submit the animals to a very stressful environment and considerably reduce their life expectancy. From this point of view, their role is controversial, even if they do make it possible for the general public to see cetaceans. The bottle-nosed dolphin and the killer whale are the species most often kept in captivity.

WHALE MEAT

The consumption of whalemeat in Iceland, Norway and Japan is very controversial

● With the use, at the beginning of the century, of a harpoon with an explosive in the head, rorquals and sperm whales were virtually wiped out.

Glossary

•ACCIDENTAL
Species or animal only rarely seen in a given region.

•BLADDER WRACK
Brown seaweed with floating bladders, common on the Atlantic and Channel coasts.

•BLOWHOLE
Cetacean nostril, situated on top of the head, through which the animal breathes.

•BLUBBER
Layer of fat under the skin of marine mammals which acts mainly as thermal insulation.

•CARNIVORES
A group of primarily meat-eating mammals. They hunt other animals.

•COSMOPOLITAN
Describes a species present in virtually all the regions of the world.

•COURTSHIP DISPLAY
Special behaviour by which males win females and repel rivals.

•ECHOLOCATION
System using sonar for fixing your position.

•GREGARIOUS
Describes animals living in a group.

•HAREM
Group of females dominated by a single male.

•KRILL
Swimming shrimp-like animals living in huge shoals in cold seas. The food of whalebone whales.

•MELON
Bulge on the end of the head of dolphins and other toothed whales.

•MORPHOLOGY
Shape of an animal: its external appearance.

•PALAEONTOLOGY
Study of fossil remains of animal and plant life.

•PELAGIC
Describes a species living and swimming in the open sea, either near the surface or deep down.

•PLANKTON
Plants and animals drifting on the ocean, nearly always very small.

•POPULATION
Group of individuals belonging to the same species.

•PREDATOR
Animal which hunts live prey for food.

•QUOTA
Number of whales which may be caught, calculated by taking account of the known total number of a population.

•RESIDENT
Species confined to a given area, the opposite of a migratory species.

•SONAR
System using high frequency wavelengths (ultrasound) which bounce off obstacles in their path giving an echo. Some animals, such as dolphins and bats, find their way about and catch their prey by sonar.

•SPERMACETI
Substance contained in the sperm whale's

head. By solidifying or liquefying, it enables the animal to go deep underwater or come back up again.

•STRANDING

Occurs when a marine mammal cannot get back to the water from a beach.

•TERRITORIAL

Species attached for all or part of the year to a given territory.

Further Reading

Bonner W N, *Natural History of Seals*, Christopher Helm, 1990
Evans P, *Whales*, Whittet Books, 1990
Martin A R, *Whales and Dolphins*, Salamander, 1990
MacDonald D and Barrett P, *Collins Field Guide Mammals of Britain and Europe*, HarperCollins, London, 1993

Addresses

Greenpeace
Canonbury Villas
London N1 2PN

Whale and Dolphin Conservation Society
PO Box 981
Bath
Avon BA1 2BT

World Wide Fund for Nature
Panda House
Weyside Park
Godalming
Surrey GU7 1XR

Index

Photographic credits
6 M. Gunther/Bios (6.1), V. Bretagnolle/Bios (6.2)
7 Y. Gladu/Jacana (7.1), P.J. Dubois (7.2)
12 J. Mayet/Bios
14 J. Trotignon
16 J. Mallwitz/Wildlife/Bios
19 F. Gohier/PHO.N.E
20 T. Lafranchis/Bios
22 F.X. Pelletier/Gamma
25 F. Gohier/PHO.N.E.
26 F. Gohier/PHO.N.E

Cover illustration
François Desbordes